HAL•LEONARD

Pro Vocal

BETTER THAN KARAOKE!

WOMEN'S EDITION   **VOLUME 32**

Hits of the

G000123817

ISBN 978-1-4234-3531-0

HAL•LEONARD®
CORPORATION
7777 W. BLUEMOUND RD. P.O. BOX 13819 MILWAUKEE, WI 53213

Visit Hal Leonard Online at
www.halleonard.com

CONTENTS

At Seventeen

Words and Music by Janis Ian

Intro
Moderately

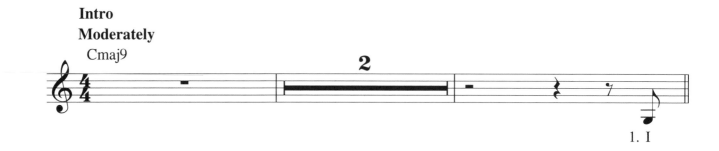

Verse

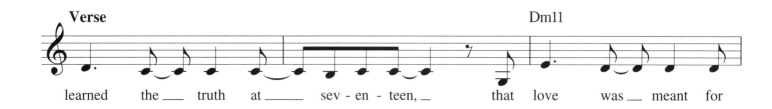

learned the truth at sev-en-teen, that love was meant for

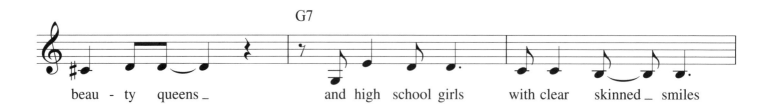

beau-ty queens and high school girls with clear skinned smiles

who mar-ried young and then re-tired.

The val-en-tines I never knew, the

Fri-day night cha-rades of youth were spent on one more

Dreams

Words and Music by Stevie Nicks

Outro-Chorus

When the rain __ wash - es _____ you clean, you'll

know. __ Oh, __ thun - der on - ly hap -

- pens __ when it's rain - in'.

Play - ers on - ly love _____ you when they're play - in'. _____

Say, __ wom - en, they will come, _____ and __ they will go. __

When the rain __ wash - es __

_____ you clean, you'll know. __ You'll

know. __ You will know. _____ Oh, __

_____ you'll __ know.

13

I Feel the Earth Move

Words and Music by Carole King

Intro
Moderately

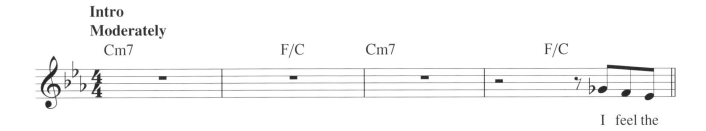

I feel the

Chorus

earth move un - der my feet. I feel the sky tum - bl - in' down. __

I feel my heart start to trem - bl - in' _____ when ev - er __

Verse

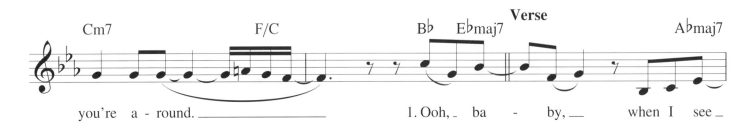

you're a - round. _____ 1. Ooh, __ ba - by, __ when I see __

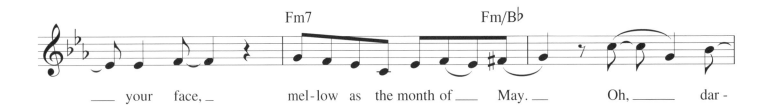

__ your face, __ mel - low as the month of __ May. __ Oh, _____ dar -

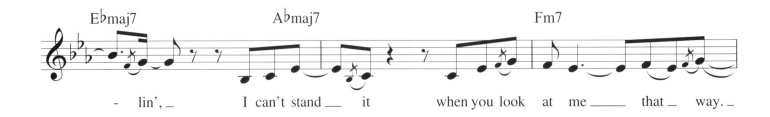

- lin', __ I can't stand __ it when you look at me _____ that __ way. __

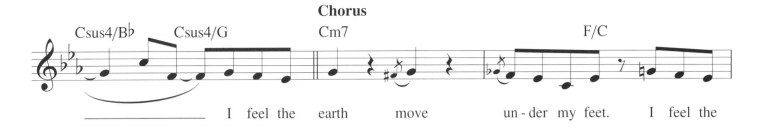

Chorus

Csus4/B♭ Csus4/G Cm7 F/C

_____ I feel the earth move un-der my feet. I feel the

Cm7 F/C F7

sky tum-bl-in' down. __ I feel my heart start to trem-bl-in' _____

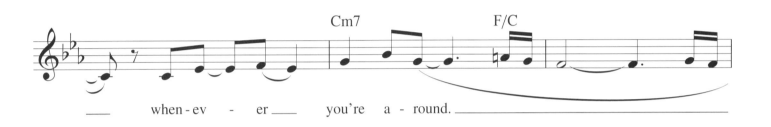

Cm7 F/C

___ when-ev - er ___ you're a - round. _____

Interlude

Cm7 F/C Cm7 **14**

_____

Verse

F B♭ E♭maj7 A♭maj7

2. Ooh, __ dar - lin', __ when you're near __ me, __ and you ten-

Fm7 A♭maj7/B♭ E♭maj7 A♭maj7

- der - ly call __ my __ name. __ I ___ know ___ that __ my e - mo-

Fm7   Csus4/B♭   Csus4/G

- tions   are some - thin' I ____ just ___ can't tame. ___ I just got to have you,

Cm7   F/C   Cm7

ba - by. ___   Ah, ah, ___ ah.   Ah, ah, ___ ah, yeah. __

Chorus

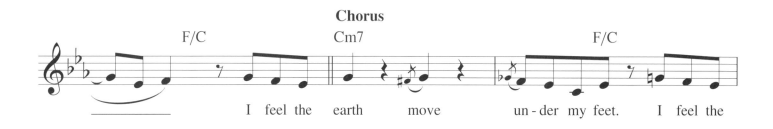

F/C   Cm7   F/C

_____ I feel the earth   move   un - der my feet.   I feel the

Cm7   F/C   Cm7

sky tum - bl - in' down, a - tum - bl - in' down. __ I feel the earth move __ un -

F/C   Cm7   F/C

- der my feet.   I feel the sky tum - bl - in' down, a - tum - bl - in' down. __ I just a -

Bridge

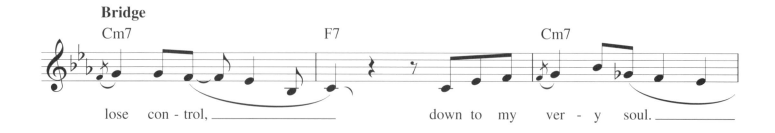

Cm7   F7   Cm7

lose con - trol, _____ down to my ver - y soul. ____

I get a   hot and cold _____ all ___ o-

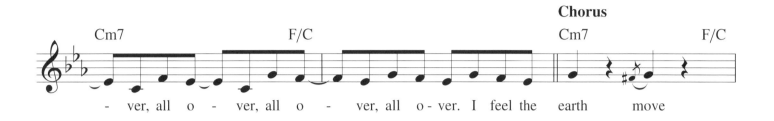

Chorus

- ver, all o - ver, all o - ver, all o - ver. I feel the earth move

un-der my feet.   I feel the   sky tum-bl-in' down, a - tum-bl-in' down. _ I feel the

earth move _   un - der my feet.   I feel the   sky tum - bl - in' down, a -

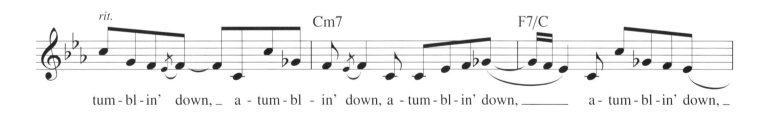

tum - bl-in' down, _ a - tum-bl - in' down, a - tum-bl-in' down, _____ a - tum-bl-in' down, _

Freely

___ tum - bl - in' ___ down. _____

Love Will Keep Us Together

Words and Music by Neil Sedaka and Howard Greenfield

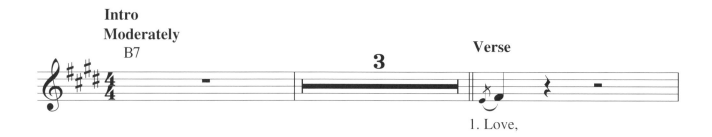

love will __ keep us to-geth - er. __ Think __ of me __ babe, __ when-ev -

er __ some sweet __ talk - in' girl __ comes a - long __

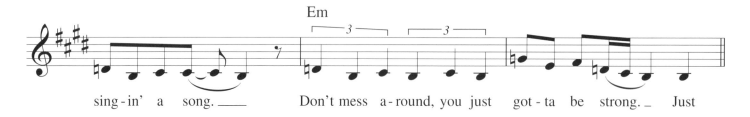

sing - in' a song. __ Don't mess a - round, you just got - ta be strong. __ Just

Chorus

stop, 'cause I __ real - ly love __ you. Stop, I've been

think - in' __ of __ you. Look in my heart, and let love __ keep us __ to-

geth - er. _____

Verse

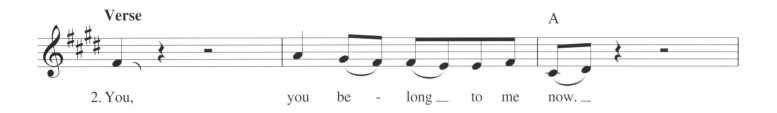

2. You,   you be - long _ to me now. _

Ain't gon - na set __ you free now   when those _ girls start

hang-in' a - round, __   talk - in' me down. __   Hear with your heart, and you

Chorus

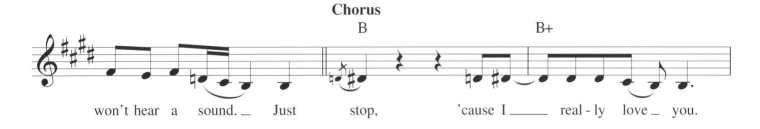

won't hear a sound. _ Just   stop,   'cause I _____ real - ly love _ you.

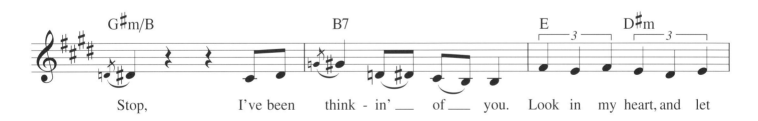

Stop,   I've been   think - in' __ of __ you. Look in my heart, and let

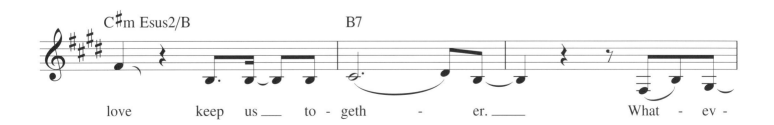

love   keep us __ to - geth - er. _____   What - ev -

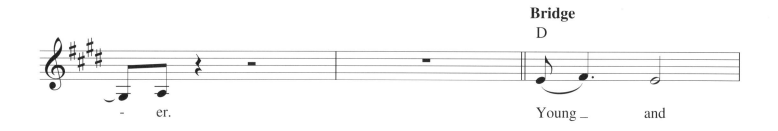

Bridge

-er.   Young __   and

beau - ti - ful, ____   well some-day, your looks will be   gone. __

When __   the oth-ers turn __ you off, ____   who'll __ be turn-in' you on? __

Verse

___   I will, ___   I will, ____   I will. __ 3. I ___   will ____ be __

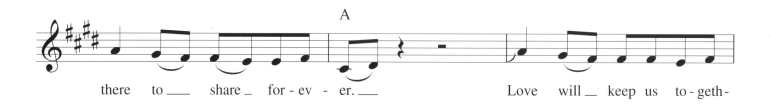

there to ___ share _ for - ev - er. ___   Love will __ keep us to - geth-

er.   I said it be - fore, _ and I'll   say it a - gain, ____   while

oth - ers pre - tend. ____   I need you now, and __   I'll need you then. __   Just

Me and Bobby McGee

Words and Music by Kris Kristofferson and Fred Foster

Intro
Moderately

1. Bust-ed flat __ in Bat-on Rouge,

wait-in' __ for a __ train. __ And I's feel-in' near as fad-ed as __ my __

jeans. __ Bob-by thumbed __ a die - sel down __

just be - fore __ it rained. ____ He rode us all the way to New Or -

leans. __ Well I pulled my har - poon __ out of __ my __

dirt-y red __ ban-dan-na. And I's play-in' soft __ while Bob-by sang the blues. __

Now. _____ Wind-shield wip-ers slap-pin' time, _ I's _

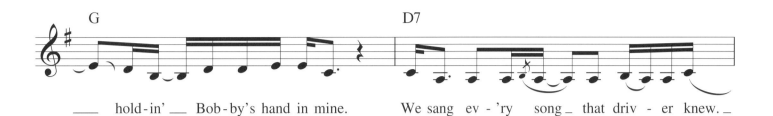

_ hold-in' _ Bob-by's hand in mine. We sang ev-'ry song_ that driv-er knew. _

Chorus

_ Well free-dom's just a-noth-er word _ for _

_ noth-in' left to lose. _ Noth-in', oh ain't noth-in', hon-ey if it ain't _

free. _____ Now, now. Well now, feel-in' good was eas-y, Lord _____

_ when he sang the blues. _ You know, feel-in' good was good e-nough _ for me. _

_____ Was good e-nough _ for me and my Bob-by _ Mc -

Verse

G   A

Gee.   2. From the Ken - tuck - y coal _ mines to the

Cal - i - for - nia sun, _ Yeah, Bob - by shared _ the se - crets of __ my __

E7

__ soul.   And through all ___ kind _ of weath - er, __ through

ev - 'ry - thing _ we done, _ yeah Bob-by, ba - by help _ me from _ this cold _

A

__ world. _   A one day up near Sa - lin - as, Lord, _

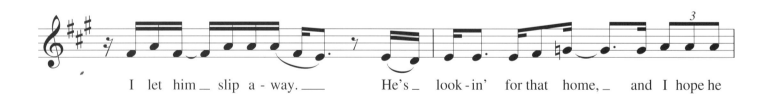

I let him _ slip a - way. __ He's _ look - in' for that home, _ and I hope he

D

finds ___ it. ___ But I'd trade all my to - mor - rows _ for one

24

na, na, na, ___ na, na. ___ La, na, na, na, na, ___ na, Bob - by ___

E

___ Mc - Gee, ___ yeah. ___ La, nay, na, ___ na, na, ___ na.

La, nay, na, ___ na, na. ___ La, nay, na, ___ na, na, ___ na, Bob - by ___

A

___ Mc - Gee, ___ yeah. ___ La, na, na. La, nay, nay, no, ___ nay, nay, no, ___ nay, now.

La, nay, nay, no, ___ nay, nay, no, ___ nay, no. Hey, now Bob - by say now Bob-by Mc-Gee, ___

E7

___ yeah. ___ La, nay, nay, no, ___ nay, nay, no, ___ nay, now. La, nay, nay, no,

___ nay, nay, no, ___ nay, nay, no, ___ nay, nay, no, ___ nay, now.

Hey now, Bob - by say now Bob - by Mc - Gee, ___

A

_____ yeah. ___ Well, _ I called _ him my lov - er, I called him my man, ___ and I

called him my lov - er just the best I ___ can. ___ Come on, ___

and it's Bob - by now, ___ it's Bob - by Mc - Gee, ___

E7

___ yeah. ___ La, ___ nay, na, ___ nay, na, ___ nay, na, ___ nay, na, ___ nay, na, ___

___ nay, na, ___ nay, na, ___ ah. ___ Hey, hey, hey, Bob - by Mc - Gee. ___

A   **13**   *Fade out*

_____ Woo.

Yesterday Once More

Words and Music by John Bettis and Richard Carpenter

Verse
Moderately

1. When I was young, I'd listen to the ra-di-o wait-in'

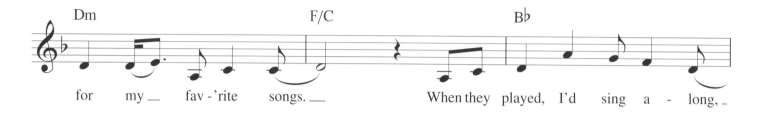

for my fav-'rite songs. When they played, I'd sing a-long,

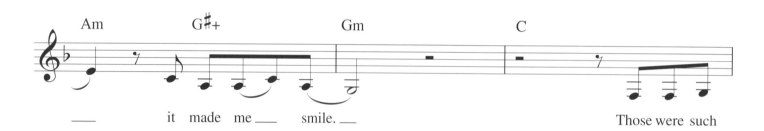

it made me smile. Those were such

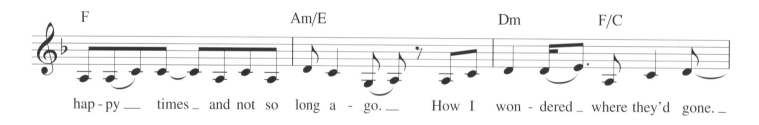

hap-py times and not so long a-go. How I won-dered where they'd gone.

But they're back a-gain, just like a long lost friend, all the

songs I loved so well. Ev-'ry sha, la, la, la, ev-'ry

woah _____ still shines. ___ Ev - 'ry

shing, a - ling, a - ling, that they're start - in' to sing ___ so fine. ___

When they get to the part ___ where he's break - ing her heart, ___ it can

real - ly make me cry. ___ Just ___ like be - fore, ___

it's yes - ter - day ___ once ___ more. _____

Verse

2. Look - in' back ___ on ___ how it was in

years gone by ___ and the good times ___ that I had, ___ makes to -

day seem ___ rath - er sad. ___ So much has ___ changed. ___

It was songs _ of _ love that I would sing to then, _ and I'd

mem - o - rize each word. _ Those old _ mel - o - dies _ still sound so

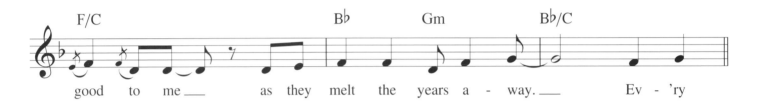

good to me _ as they melt the years a - way. _ Ev - 'ry

Chorus

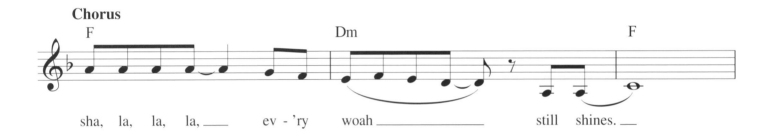

sha, la, la, la, _ ev - 'ry woah _ still shines. _

Ev -'ry shing, a - ling, a - ling, that they're start - in' to sing _ so fine. _

All my best mem - o - ries _ come back

clear - ly to me, _ some can e - ven _ make me cry. _ Just _ like be - fore, _

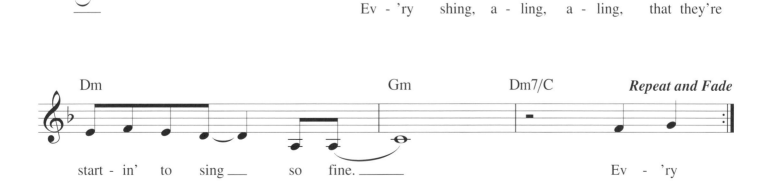

You're So Vain

Words and Music by Carly Simon

walked in - to a par - ty like you were walk - in' on - to ___ a ___ yacht. ___

___ You hat stra - te - gi - c'lly dipped be - low ___ one eye, ___ your

scarf, it was ap - ri - cot. ___ You had one eye in the mir -

- ror as ___ you watched your - self ___ ga - votte. ___

___ And all ___ of the girls ___ dreamed that they'd ___ be your part - ner, they'd ___

Chorus

____ be your part - ner and... You're _ so ___ vain. ___ You

prob -'bly think this song is a - bout ___ you. You're _ so ___ vain. ___ I'll

bet you think this song is a - bout __ you. Don't _ you? Don't ___ you? ___ 2.Well you ___

Verse

____ had me sev -'ral years ____ a - go ___ when I was still quite _ na - ive. ___

____ When you said ___ that we made _ such a pret - ty pair __ and

that you would nev - er ___ leave. ___ But you gave a - way ____ the things _

_____ you loved, __ and one of them __ was me. __

Bridge

____ I ___ had some dreams, _ they were clouds ____ in my cof -fee, clouds _

Chorus

____ in my cof - fee and... You're _ so ___ vain. ___ You

33

Goodbye to Love

Words and Music by Richard Carpenter and John Bettis

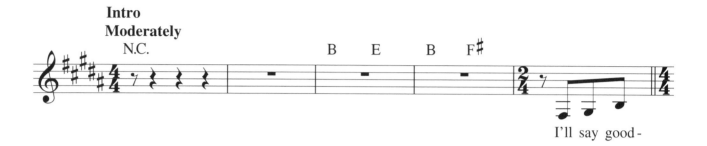

I'll say good-

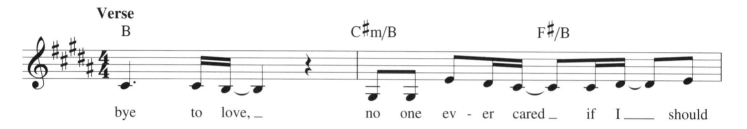

bye to love, no one ev - er cared if I should

live or die. Time and time a - gain the chance for

love has passed me by, and all I know of love is how to live with-out

it. I just can't seem to find it.

So I've made my mind up, I must live my life a - lone. And

Bridge

What lies in the fu - ture is a mys - t'ry to us ___ all.

No one can pre - dict ___ the ___ wheel of for - tune as it falls.

There may come a time ___ when I will see that I've ___ been wrong, but for

Verse

now this is my ___ song, _____ and it's good - bye to love. _____

I'll say good - bye to love. _____

Outro

Ah. _____

Ah, _____

Repeat Four Times and Fade

ah. _____

Pro Vocal® Series
Songbook & Sound-Alike CD
Sing 8 Chart-Topping Songs with a Professional Band

Whether you're a karaoke singer or an auditioning professional, the Pro Vocal® series is for you! Unlike most karaoke packs, each book in the ProVocal Series contains the lyrics, melody, and chord symbols for eight hit songs. The CD contains demos for listening, and separate backing tracks so you can sing along. The CD is playable on any CD player, but it is also enhanced so PC and Mac computer users can adjust the recording to any pitch without changing the tempo! Perfect for home rehearsal, parties, auditions, corporate events, and gigs without a backup band.

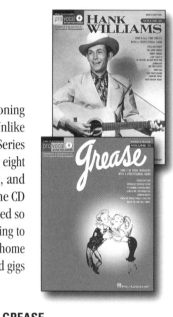

BROADWAY SONGS
00740247 Women's Edition.........................$12.95
00740248 Men's Edition.............................$12.95

MICHAEL BUBLÉ
00740362 ....$14.95

CHRISTMAS STANDARDS
00740299 Women's Edition.........................$12.95
00740298 Men's Edition.............................$12.95

KELLY CLARKSON
00740377 ....$14.95

PATSY CLINE
00740374 ....$14.95

CONTEMPORARY HITS
00740246 Women's Edition.........................$12.95
00740251 Men's Edition.............................$12.95

DISCO FEVER
00740281 Women's Edition.........................$12.95
00740282 Men's Edition.............................$12.95

DISNEY'S BEST
00740344 Women's Edition.........................$14.95
00740345 Men's Edition.............................$14.95

DISNEY FAVORITES
00740342 Women's Edition.........................$14.95
00740343 Men's Edition.............................$14.95

'80S GOLD
00740277 Women's Edition.........................$12.95
00740278 Men's Edition.............................$12.95

ELLA FITZGERALD
00740378..$14.95

GREASE
00740369 Women's Edition.........................$14.95
00740370 Men's Edition.............................$14.95

JOSH GROBAN
00740371 ....$17.95

HIGH SCHOOL MUSICAL 1 & 2
00740360 Women's Edition.........................$14.95
00740361 Men's Edition.............................$14.95

HANNAH MONTANA
00740375 ....$14.95

HIP-HOP HITS
00740368 Men's Edition.............................$14.95

HITS OF THE '70S
00740384 Women's Edition.........................$14.95
00740383 Men's Edition $14.95

JAZZ BALLADS
00740353 Women's Edition.........................$12.95

JAZZ FAVORITES
00740354 Women's Edition.........................$12.95

JAZZ STANDARDS
00740249 Women's Edition.........................$12.95
00740250 Men's Edition.............................$12.95

JAZZ VOCAL STANDARDS
0074037 Women's Edition..........................$14.95

Prices, contents, & availability subject to change without notice.
Disney charaters and artwork © Disney Enterprises, Inc.

For More Information, See Your Local Music Dealer,
Or Write To:

HAL•LEONARD®
CORPORATION
7777 W. Bluemound Rd. P.O. Box 13819 Milwaukee, WI 53213

MOVIE SONGS
00740365 Women's Edition.........................$14.95
00740366 Men's Edition.............................$14.95

MUSICALS OF BOUBLIL & SCHÖNBERG
00740350 Women's Edition.........................$14.95
00740351 Men's Edition.............................$14.95

ELVIS PRESLEY
00740333 Volume 1..................................$14.95
00740335 Volume 2..................................$14.95

R&B SUPER HITS
00740279 Women's Edition.........................$12.95
00740280 Men's Edition.............................$12.95

FRANK SINATRA CLASSICS
00740347 ....$14.95

FRANK SINATRA STANDARDS
00740346 ....$14.95

TORCH SONGS
00740363 Women's Edition.........................$12.95
00740364 Men's Edition.............................$12.95

TOP HITS
00740380 Women's Edition.........................$14.95

ANDREW LLOYD WEBBER
00740348 Women's Edition.........................$14.95
00740349 Men's Edition.............................$14.95

WEDDING GEMS
00740309 Book/CD Pack Women's Edition.............$12.95
00740310 Book/CD Pack Men's Edition................$12.95
00740311 Duets Edition.................................$12.95

HANK WILLIAMS
00740386 ....$14.95

0308

Visit Hal Leonard online at www.halleonard.com